The History
Of
SQUARE DANCING

THE HISTORY
Of
SQUARE DANCING

by S. Foster Damon

BARRE GAZETTE
BARRE, MASSACHUSETTS
1957

Foreword

TODAY in America we find ourselves in a great period of square dancing. These old American folk-dances, which have never died out, have revived and spread from backwoods and mountains and plains into the cities again. Yet nothing seems to be known whence they came originally and how they developed into what they are. For some years now, I have been gathering information from old dance-books, town-histories, travellers' chronicles, newspapers, novels of the old times, even poetry and sheet-music, with results which have fitted together into an outline-history of this forgotten phase of our culture. This history is not unamusing, pivoting as it does, now upon some great revolution, and again upon so trivial a matter as a change of style in ladies' skirts. For the history of square-dancing is an expression of the ever-changing time-spirit.

Anthropologists report that the great apes have been observed dancing in lines and circles. If this be so, folk-dancing is probably older than mankind. Certainly in man's own half-billion years, folk-dancing has spread everywhere, so that there is not a step, not a formation, probably not a figure, which may not be found somewhere else on the face of the globe. No tribe, no nation, can now claim to have originated anything, especially as the chronicles for this world-wide event were never kept. But the movement which produced American square - dancing emerged into the light of history on March 19, 1651; for on that day was published the first English dance-book, John Playford's epochal *English Dancing-Master*.

It was a Puritan publication, issued while the young commonwealth was involved in its first wars. But revolutionists must dance; and when they defy the rest of the world (as the Puritans did in killing their king), they dance their own national dances. Playford's book met that demand. It published the gay, simple native dances with their traditional tunes, to fill the vacuum left by

1

the disappearance of the imported, complicated dances favored by the court. In the ballroom as on the battlefield, the people routed the crown. Playford's book was an enormous success: it went through seventeen editions between 1651 and 1728, each edition being altered and enlarged until the original 104 dances had swollen to 918.

At this point, one should take time out to explain that the Puritans approved of dancing and enjoyed it thoroughly.[1] This indubitable fact goes against that venerable vulgar error which insists that they were blue-nosed kill-joys, who hated all fun and passed (untraceable) laws against music. But facts are facts. The attitude of the Puritans was that of their favorite authors, Spenser, Milton, and the stricter Bunyan, in whose works all good people dance, from the angels down. Cromwell, famous as a music-lover (during whose rule opera was started in England), introduced "mixt dancing" at the wedding of his daughter Frances on November 11, 1657; doubtless they did dances out of Playford's recent book. Playford himself was the first British publisher to specialize in music. During the Puritan period he issued twenty-one items between 1651 and 1659 (listed by

[1]See Percy A. Scholes's *The Puritans and Music in England and New England,* London, 1934, for overwhelming evidence of the Puritans' love of music and dancing. He also lists and demolishes the statements of those who for so long have parroted the anti-Puritan satires as though they were history.

Scholes) : dance-books, song-books, the works of
the leading composers, and instruction-books. John
Locke, the apostle of common sense, the great
Whig philosopher, whose works were kept next the
Bible, wrote (and I quote from an old Boston
dance-book) :[2]

> Nothing appears to me to give the children so much
> becoming confidence and behaviour, and so to raise them
> to the conversation of those above their age, as dancing.
> I think they should be taught to dance as soon as they are
> capable of learning it;   for, (though this consists only of
> outward gracefulness of motion, yet, I know not how, it gives
> children manly thoughts and carriage more than any thing.

In this country, the high priest of Boston, the
Reverend John Cotton, specifically approved of
dancing, — "yea, though mixt," though both
Increase and Cotton Mather preferred it "unmixt."
They seem, however, to have been pretty much
in the minority, as the latter, in his *Cloud of
Witnesses* (1700?), complained that he had
heard "not so much as one word from my English
Nonconformists" against the Boston balls, where
the dances were certainly not solos. Nor can we
imagine a segregation of sexes around the maypole
in Charlestown, which, Judge Sewall fumed in
1687, was cut down only to be replaced by a bigger
one. It is also certain that Boston had its dancing
schools in the last third of the seventeenth cen-

[2] *A Selection of Cotillions & Country-Dances.* Printed by J. T.
Buckingham for the Compiler. [Boston] 1808, p. 3.

tury.[3] Presently newly appointed ministers were
giving "Ordination Balls." The earliest yet traced
was given by the Reverend Timothy Edwards
(father of the famous Jonathan) in 1694. In
her nostalgic *Old Town Folks*, Harriet Beecher
Stowe wondered how the idea ever got started that
the New England clergy objected to dancing; and
recent researchers have been surprised to make the
same discovery.[4]

[3] Unfortunately for the historian, these early dancing-masters
never advertised; consequently, we learn about them only when
they got into trouble. Carl Bridenbaugh (*Cities in the Wilderness*,
pp. 117-8) has spotted two. The first, in 1672, was "put down,"
no explanation available. The second, in 1681, was started by
Monsieur Henri Sherlot, "a person of very insolent & ill fame,
that Raves & Scoffes at Religion." He was ordered out of town,
whereupon Increase Mather wrote his *Arrow against Profane and
Promiscuous Dancing*. He reissued it in 1685, when another vaga-
bond, Francis Stepney, chose Lecture Day for his classes and
otherwise defied the ministry, then fled town ahead of his creditors.
He became the first dancing master in New York, only to be
stopped when his bad reputation caught up with him. But who
ran the Boston dancing-school in 1708, when Cotton Mather
complained that parents were more concerned with it than
with their children's souls? He was shocked again in 1711 when
the youngsters of his congregation held "a Frolick, a revelling
Feast, and Ball" on—here lay the real crime—on Christmas night.
In 1712, George Brownell (Franklin's teacher) advertised dancing
among the things he taught; in 1714 Edward Enstone (organist
at King's Chapel) advertised the same; in 1716 they were running
rival advertisements in the *Boston Newsletter*. (Enstone won, and
Brownell removed to New York.) Then there was Mr. Gatchell,
whose place was stoned on February 28, 1723, by some boys who
were "deny'd Admittance"; otherwise we should not know about
him. He was followed by Ephraim Turner (father of William
Turner, the musician) and Peter Pelham (step-father of Copley,
the painter). There is no point in continuing the list further.

[4] The Great Awakening for a time produced a change of attitude, as Percy Scholes has pointed out. In 1744, Dr. Alexander
Hamilton found that Whitefield's influence had stopped all assemblies and much music in Philadelphia; but at Boston, things were

Of course, the Puritans had a justification for their approval. Dancing taught manners, and manners were a minor branch of morals. It was as simple as that. We may smile condescendingly at our ancestors for devising moral reasons for something that is plain fun; but if anybody has observed how square-dancing improves the morale of underprivileged children (as I have), he will know just what the wise old Puritans also knew.

Playford's dances were not only national; they were also deliberately democratic. The performers were no longer nominated ladies and gentlemen but simply "men" and "women." But more than that: the type of dance which already was most popular was that in which everybody dances with everybody else, regardless of rank. This was the

different. On August 16, he noted: "Assemblies of the gayer sort are frequent here; the gentlemen and ladys meeting almost every week att consorts of musick and balls. I was present att two or three such and saw as fine a ring of ladys, as good dancing, and heard musick as elegant as I had been witness to any where. . . I saw not one prude while I was here." (Carl Bridenbaugh, *Gentleman's Progress,* Chapel Hill, 1949, p. 146.)

Hangovers from this severity doubtless account for the occasional (and invariably futile) clerical opposition to dancing one meets in the novels. In Sylvester Judd's *Margaret* (1845) a novel about American country life between 1783 and 1800, a minister tries in vain to stop a Thanksgiving dance. In George M. Baker's *Running Wild* (1874), Deacon Thompson does not object, as expected, to a dance in his own house. In Mary Wilkins Freeman's *Madelon* (1896), the orthodox minister (who has lost most of his congregation) does not permit his daughter to dance, though it may be added that she does, and does it very well.

For a southern example, see George W. Harris's *Sut Lovingood's Yarns,* New York [1867], where a "hard-shell preacher" tries to break up Bart Davis's' dance, and gets mobbed.

"longways" (soon to be known as the "country-dance"), formed in two lines facing each other, as in our Virginia Reel. Any couple can join in at the foot at any time; and even if they don't know the dance, they will by the time they reach the top, when it is their turn to go down the line.

This "longways," like all subsequent square-dancing, was thus a community game, and as such was differentiated from all other types of dances: the hornpipes and other solos, which are exhibitions of individual skill; and the couple-dances, which are courtship more or less disguised as deportment.

The question of precedence (which complicated the formation of courtly dances very much) naturally came up, as the elite would resent standing below persons of lower social rank. But the problem was solved democratically. The first place was reserved for brides or distinguished guests. In informal parties, the couples simply fell in below as they arrived. In formal assemblies, it was the custom for the ladies to draw lots for their places that evening, and frequently for their partners as well.

A study of the successive editions of Playford shows the development and triumph of the long-ways, until it had virtually ousted all other dances whatsoever. In the first edition of 1651, there are thirty-eight longways "for as many as will" and forty-one for a limited number of couples. The dancers do not always progress down the line. There are also fourteen rounds (or circle dances), three squares, and one for a single line. In the last edition (1721, 1728), 904 of the 918 dances are longways; and there are only two squares. The longways thus became *the* dance of both high and low society.[5]

As soon as the English ceased to be the Red Menace of Europe and returned to international respectability by restoring the throne to its legitimate heir, Charles II, these "English dances" swept

[5] Apparently the democratic longways was fairly recent, as it is not described in Sir John Davies's brilliant poem on dancing, *Orchestra* (1596). According to him, the earliest English dances were "a thousand brawles" or branles; then came the rounds (which he calls "country dances"), the "winding heyes," and rings around trees. The first formal dances were the solemn spondaic "measures," after which followed the livelier galliards, corantoes, and lavoltas. Thus the longways must have risen to popularity in the ensuing half-century.

For my statistics about Playford, I rely on Cecil J. Sharp's *Country Dance Book*, Pts. II-IV, VI. The seventeen editions of Playford were: 1651, 1652, 1665, 1670, 1675, 1679, 1686, 1690, 1695, 1698, 1701, 1703, 1707, 1709, 1713, 1716, 1721, (Pt. II and III, 1728).

As far as I know, none of the dances in the 1651 Playford have survived. Several of them have been revived, however, in this century, through the efforts of Cecil J. Sharp; and as the groups devoted to these early English dances (chiefly in college communities) have flourished for some forty years, we may safely assume that the dances are still fun.

At least one of the 1651 tunes is still used: "Dargason, or Sedany," which we know today under its 18th century title, the "Irish Washerwoman." The pre-Shakesperean "Green Sleeves" is also to be heard occasionally; it is found in the later editions of Playford.

the continent and became a craze.[6] They were so simple, so fresh and gay, so Arcadian! All the composers wrote country-dances, even Beethoven, who used one of his tunes again for the last movement of the Heroic Symphony.

The French adapted the name "country-dance" as "contre-danse," a term which later got translated back into English as "contra-dance," or "contra" for short. They also developed a type of their own. Their sense of form was not satisfied with the long double line of an indefinite number of couples, so they concentrated on the square limited to four couples. These squares were known at first as "French contra-dances," or more simply as "French dances"; then, as they were still rural in concept, they acquired the name "cotillon" (anglicized as "cotillion") meaning a peasant girl's petticoat. The inspiration may have come from their little girls' ring-around-a-rosy:

> Ma commère, quand je danse,
> Mon cotillon va-t-il bien?
> Il va de çi, il va de ça
> Comme le queue de notre chat.[7]

These French squares were the origin of our own squares, and have nothing to do with the modern

---

[6] For details, see Curt Sachs, *World History of the Dance,* New York, 1937, pp. 397-401, 414-24.

[7] The French call "queue de chat" (half promenade, half right and left) may also come from this rhyme.

"german" or "cotillion," a dance characterized by the distribution of favors.[8]

The contras were so simple that anybody could learn them while they were being danced; but the squares were more complicated, and had to be memorized beforehand. Consequently, the French dances were considered the height of elegance, and were performed after the opening minuets, but before the company settled down to an evening of straight longways dances.

In the *Spectator* for May 17, 1711, is a glimpse of a London dancing-school. It is written in the character of the Indignant Father, concerned over his darling daughter; thus the essay ridicules gently those moralists who objected to dancing. The Father approved wholly of the "French Dancing" at the start, and solemnly endorsed "Hunt the Squirrel" (a dance still performed in America)[9] for its ethical content. (The gentleman pursues the lady; but when he turns back, she pursues him.) However, he was shocked by the hearty freedom of the other country-dances.

[8] After the French Quadrille was introduced into England in 1815, the word "quadrille" replaced "cotillion," which, however, continued for long to be used in America, as the English travellers complained. The "German Cotillion" was brought to New York in 1844, where, to avoid confusion, it was known simply as the "German." (Allen Dodsworth, *Dancing*, New York, 1885, p. 145.) Later it was also called "the cotillion."

[9] For the sake of showing how an old dance survives in this

They very often made use of a most impudent and lascivious Step called *Setting,* which I know not how to describe
to you, but by telling you that it is the very Reverse of *Back
to Back.* At last an impudent young Dog bid the Fiddlers
play a Dance called Mol. Pately, and after having made two
or three Capers, ran to his Partner, locked his Arms in hers,
and whisked her round cleverly above Ground in such man-
ner that I, who sat upon one of the lowest Benches, saw
further above her Shoe than I think fit to acquaint you with.
I could no longer endure these Enormities, wherefore just
as my Girl was going to be made a Whirligig, I ran in,
seized on the Child, and carried her home.

country, I have traced "Chase the Squirrel" through the following
works:

Clement Weeks, ms. 1783. "Chase the Squirrel."

John H. Ives, *Twenty Four Figures,* New Haven 1800. "The
Chase."

Saltator, *Treatise on Dancing,* Boston, 1802. "Heathen
Mythology." This title is the name of the seventeenth century
tune, also known as "The Hunting of the Hare."

Select Collection, Otsego, 1808. "Hare Hunt."

Elias Howe, *Howe's Complete Ball-Room Hand-Book,* Boston,
1858. "Chase (or Hunt) the Squirrel." It is also included
in Howe's subsequent publications.

Elias Howe, *Howe's New American Dancing Master,* Boston,
1882. "Chase the Lady; or Chase (or Hunt) the Squirrel.
Tune: The Cuckoo."

Larry Chittenden, "Cowboy's Christmas Ball" (*Ranch Verses,*
New York, 1893) mentions "Chase the Squirrel" as a call.

J. M. French, *Prompter's Hand Book,* New York, 1893.
"Chase the Squirrel."

Elizabeth Burchenal, *American Country Dances,* Boston, 1918.
"Chase the Squirrel."

David Cort, "Swing Your Partner" (*Bookman,* August, 1927)
lists "Chase the Squirrel."

Foster's Square Dances [cards for callers], Denver, 1942.
"Chase the Squirrel." The contra has now folded up into a
square.

Durward Maddocks, *Swing Your Partners,* New York, 1941.
"Chase the Squirrel." The dance is now reduced to a figure
for two couples, repeated round the square. The call goes.
Chase the squirrel round the two;
Lady goes round and gent cuts through.
Now back around the same old track;
The gent goes around and the lady cuts back.

The *Spectator's* comment on this letter hedges politely about the moral problem. He disapproves of "those kissing Dances in which Will Honeycomb assures me they are obliged to dwell almost a Minute on the Fair One's lips, or they will be too quick for the Musick, and dance quite out of Time." He also admits that in country-dancing "the greatest Familiarities between the two Sexes on this Occasion may sometimes produce very dangerous Consequences," and dwells a lurid moment on the possibilities.

But as this kind of Dance is the particular Invention of our own Country, and as everyone is more or less a Proficient in it, I would not Discountenance it; but rather suppose it may be practised innocently by others, as well as my Self, who am often Partner to my landlady's Eldest Daughter.

It is rather amusing to find the Indignant Father's attitude repeated sixty years later by the jealous lover Faulkland in Sheridan's *Rivals* (1775); he is distressed to learn that his Julia has been dancing in his absence.

A minuet I could have forgiven—I should not have minded that — I say I should not have regarded a minuet — but *country-dances!*—Z——ds! had she made one in a *cotillion* I believe I could have forgiven even that—but to be monkey-led for a night!—to run the gauntlet through a string of amorous palming puppies!—to show paces like a managed filly!—O Jack, there never can be but *one* man in the world whom a truly modest and delicate woman ought to pair with in a country-dance; and even then, the rest of the couples should be her great uncles and aunts!

His attitude was just the reverse of Bob Acres in

the same play: he was "accounted a good stick" in a country-dance, but cursed the inventor of cotillions. For by this time, the latest squares from France were becoming something of a craze. In 1790, Tam O'Shanter's witches scorned the "cotillon brent new frae France." and it is worth mentioning that in Jane Austen's *Northanger Abbey*, the fashionable Tilney youngsters do not arrive at the cotillion ball until the cotillions are over. Nevertheless, the squares were to outrival the contras, as we shall see.

What was done in the capital was done, sooner or later, in the colonies; and in the colonies, what was done in town was soon done in the country. (Folk-lore students are still being surprised and a bit chagrined to learn that much folk-material originated in the upper classes.) And so, from the dancing-schools in the cities the new dances spread to the villages, where, according to the historian of Northampton, they held their junkets at weddings, Thanksgiving, quilting-bees, and the conclusion of sleigh-rides, on which the fiddler was taken along. "Reels, jigs, and contra-dances were most in vogue," says the historian of Norwich, Connecticut; "the hornpipe and rigadoon were attempted only by a select few; cotillions were growing in favor; the minuet much admired." The Virginians, said the Reverend Andrew Burna-

by, were "immoderately fond of dancing," which
was almost their only amusement; and when the
company was "pretty well tired with country
dances," they took to jigs, which were tests of
endurance. It is surprising to find the Shakes-
perean corante, which had long since died out in
Europe, described in Saltator's *Treatise on Dancing*,
Boston, 1802, with the note that it is "very pleasant for private parties or for public performance."

The American Revolution was conservative: a
preserving of the *status quo* by clinging to the
traditional English liberties. The division with
the mother-country was political only, not cultural. Therefore the Americans did not invent a
new type of dance, but expressed their revolutionary ardor in new dances of the old type. Already
they had developed quite a corpus of their own
country-dances.[10] The new ones, inspired by the
war, were, as the Marquis de Chastellux noted in
1780, "related to politics"; he names "The Success
of the Campaign," "The Defeat of Burgoyne,"

[10] The evidence lies in the manuscript dance-books, such as those
of Clement Weeks (1783) and Nancy Shepley (ca. 1795), both at
the American Antiquarian Society, and of Asa Willcox (1793) at
the Newbury Library, and an unauthored one, *incipit* "Love in the
Village," of the same period, at the Rhode Island Historical
Society. All four are obviously drawn from the same tradition;
and most of their dances are not found abroad. On the other hand,
Cantelo's *Twenty Four American Country Dances,* London 1785,
consists entirely of dances invented by the invading British—
dances none of which took; neither did those in *Twenty-Four
Fashionable Country Dances for the Year* 1799, London printed,
Boston reprinted.

and "Clinton's Retreat."[11] There was also an added regard for cotillions, the dances of our ally, France.

The formal assemblies were carefully organized entertainments, often with printed rules. At Newport in 1747, the sixteenth of the (ms.) dance regulations reads:

> With respect to Dancing of Minuets, the Gentlemen shall dance with such Ladies As the Master of Ceremonies shall Appoint And of Sett or Cuntrey dances, the usual Method of drawing numbers Shall be Observed (the first Numbers to have the Precedency) with this priviledge to the Master of the Ceremonies that he shall always chuse his own Partner and open the Ball.[12]

In 1782, an unidentified Yale tutor went to Albany, where on March 13, he attended a dance. The gentlemen went for their partners in a sleigh provided for the purpose. When they arrived, the drawing took place immediately.

> The ball was opened with a minuet, and a country dance was immediately called.[13] They succeeded each other till supper, which was a good one, but plain. A few cotillions were then danced, with one or two reels, and the whole closed

---

[11] Catherine Perry Hargrave ("The Playing Cards of Puritan New England," *Old-Time New England,* April 1928) also mentions "The Military Assembly," "The Success of the Campaign," "The Defeat of Burgoyne," and "The Retreat of Clinton"—dances printed on playing cards. Other revolutionary titles are "Stoney Point," "Hessian Camp," and "Baron Steuben."

[12] "Dance Regulations of 1747" *R. I. Hist. Soc. Coll.,* XXIII, 56-9, April, 1930.

[13] "Called" probably means "announced," as calling in the modern sense does not seem to have been invented as yet.

with a set of country dances. Broke up about three, and each
retired with his partner.[14]

In 1785, a young Englishman, Robert Hunter,
after riding forty-five miles in a heavy rain,
attended an assembly in New Haven on October
20. The master of ceremonies introduced him to
Miss Betsey Beers, with whom he "walked a
minuet"; then he danced country-dances with
Miss Law, the judge's daughter. At ten they were
regaled with tea, coffee, and "an elegant supper";
then from eleven until one, they danced "Cotillions, jigs, and Scotch reels."

At the Providence assemblies of 1792, the dance
began with minuets at six o'clock. At seven the
drawings were held. The gentlemen's places were
those for the entire evening; they also drew for
partners for the first three country-dances, after
which they were apparently free to choose as they
would. From seven until midnight, nothing but
contras were permitted, though there was doubtless an hour out for supper. After midnight, the
last hour was limited strictly to minuets and cotillions.

Elias Howe's reminiscenses of this period (in
Howe's Complete Ball-Room Hand-Book, Boston,
1858) omit the cotillions, but otherwise are

[14]For this account, and the following one of Robert Hunter, see
Lea S. Luquer's "An Old-Time Assembly," *Old-Time New England,* XLI, 89-91, April-June, 1951.

important, as he names dances and comments on the steps.

Fifty years ago or more, the Country Dance was the only one danced in this country, except in the cities and large towns, where several fancy dances were occasionally performed; but even in these places the country dance reigned triumphant.

The dances that were at that time the most fashionable were: "The Fisher's Hornpipe," "Chorus Jig," "Sir Rodger deCoverly," "The Cushion Dance" [a kissing dance], "Money Musk," "Speed the Plough," "The Devil's Dream," "College Hornpipe," "Rustic Reel," "Reel fore and after or a straight four," "Durang's Hornpipe," "The Sailor's Hornpipe," &c.

It was then the custom to take all the steps in each of the different dances, and to introduce the "Pigeon's Wing" or some other flourish, as often as possible; dancers at that time often boasted that they "put in so much work" as to wear out a pair of dancing slippers in one evening. The walking or sliding through the different changes, so fashionable at the present day, would have filled our forefathers with horror and disgust.

Remnants of these old steps are still to be found in the New England countryside.

The atheistic Monsieur Sherlot, briefly of Boston, was but the first French dancing-master known over here; others followed soon. Chateaubriand, in his search for primitive culture, claimed even to have found one in the American wilderness: a Monsieur Violet, dancing-master to the Iroquois, who took his pay in beaver skins and bear hams. After the Revolution there was quite an influx of them. But none was more important than the now forgotten native, John Griffith (later Grif-

fiths), author of the first dance-book published
in America, and the most influential dancing-
master of his generation.

The career of an itinerant is not easy to trace.
Margot Mayo informs me that "Mr. Griffiths"
advertised a public ball every fortnight "in his
Dancing-School, the City Assembly Room in the
Broadway" (*New York Packet,* Jan. 2, 1786).
After what may have been several seasons in New
York, he went north. In the spring of 1787 he
was at Hartford, where he remained for a season,
then moved on to Norwich, and probably covered
the towns nearby. In February, 1788, he established
himself at Providence, where on May 10 his first
book was published. In the fall he went on to Boston, where he remained for a few years. By 1794 he
was teaching at Northampton, Amherst, and
probably Greenfield. Besides pamphlets issued at
Greenfield and Northampton in 1794, he published
another at Hartford in 1797. There are indications
that he also taught in New Jersey and New York.
Sonneck places him as far south as Charleston,
South Carolina.[15] What became of him, nobody
knows.

*A Collection of the newest and most fashionable
country dances and cotillions, the greater part by
Mr. John Griffith, dancing-master, in Providence*

[15] Oscar G. T. Sonneck and William T. Upton, *A Bibliography
of Early Secular American Music,* Washington, 1945, p. 507.

stands approximately halfway between the first
edition of Playford and our own times. But it is
a modern book: most of the dances could be done
today, with the caller using Griffiths' own words:
"cast off," "right and left," "right and left all
round," "down the middle," "four hands round,"
and the like. French terms still in use today are also
to be found here, already anglicized: "promenade,"
"balance" (still sometimes pronounced "bal-
ansay"), "'chassee" (always pronounced "sashay"
today; it is actually spelled "sasha" in John Bur-
bank's *New Collection of Country Dances,*
Brookfield, 1799). Griffiths' "allemande," how
ever, signifies the *pas allemande* (in which the lady
pirouettes under the gentleman's arm), and not
the ordinary left- or right-hand turn used today.
His "grand moline" is our "star": "Star—Mill—
Windmill — Moulinet" are equivalent terms,
according to Al Muller's *All-American Square
Dances,* New York, 1941, p. 6. The only obsolete
term seems to be "set," and that has gone out only
since Lewis Carroll described his "Lobster Quadrille."[16] And one of the dances — "Fisher's
Hornpipe" — is still danced.

[16] "Setting" or "footing it" disappeared because it became identified with "balancing." In the original balance, one stepped on the
right foot and kicked the left across, then repeated, starting on
the left foot. In setting, the left was crossed over and the weight
rested momentarily on the left toes. When the quadrilles came in,
balancing was considered too energetic; therefore a simple forward
and back was substituted. This substitute step is still used in

Unfortunately for the historian, Griffith did not collect the dances everybody did, but instead, a lot of new dances he hoped to introduce, particularly a number of his own invention. There are twenty-nine country-dances, followed by thirteen cotillions. The latter probably came direct from France, as in the *Boston Independent Chronicle* for December 11, 1788, he advertised that he taught "new Cotillions—which have been but four months invented in Paris — and a Solo-Minuet which was never before danced in America — to Musick made by the celebrated Mr. Fisher."[17]

In 1794, he issued his second dance-book at Northampton (advertised in the *Hampshire Gazette,* December 3, 1794, as "Just Published"). It was a complete rewriting, in which he retained only four of the dances in his first book: "Constancy," "Fisher's Hornpipe," "Griffith's Fancy," and "The Young Widow." It opens with nine new cotillions, which have such revolutionary titles as "Ca Ira" and "La Guilliotine" [*sic*]. Thirty-two country-dances follow. It was this book which proved so influential.

The importance of Griffiths lies not so much in his unusual activity, or his pioneering in small

the west. Ralph Page has recently protested against the vigor which the easterners put into the kick-balance.

[17] Johann Christian Fischer (b. 1733) came to London about 1780 and settled there in 1790. His minuet was a great hit, as was also his hornpipe.

towns which never had a dancing-master before, as in the fact that he published books; and his Northampton collection was freely drawn on and even pirated by others. A list of his publications (probably incomplete, as few copies have survived, and several titles are known only from newspaper advertisements) with the piracies will show what happened.

A Collection of the newest and most fashionable country dances and cotillions. The greater part by Mr. John Griffith, dancing-master, in Providence. Providence, 1788. RIHS.

A Collection of the newest cotillions and country dances; principally composed by John Griffiths, dancing-master. To which is added, Instances of ill manners, to be carefully avoided by youth of both sexes. Northampton [1794].   MHS, NYHS, Forbes.

—The same, Greenfield, 1794   [Sonneck-Upton p. 76.]

—The same, Hartford, 1797.   [Evans.]

The Sky Lark. Second Worcester edition. Worcester, 1797. [The appendix is a reprint of Griffiths 1794, filled out with six additional dances.] AAS,BPL.

The Gentleman & Lady's Companion. Norwich, 1798. [A piracy of Griffiths 1794.]   L. C. Watkinson Lib.

—The same, Second Edition. Stonington-Port, 1798.
                                        AAS, JCB

The Echo; or, Federal Songster. Brookfield, [1798]. [Contains five cotillions and seventeen country-dances selected from Griffiths 1794.]   AAS

The Gentleman & Lady's Companion. Newport, 1799. [Third edition of this piracy.]   Newport Hist. Soc.

A Collection of contra dances. Walpole [N.H.], 1799.
[The last ten dances are taken from Griffiths 1794.]
AAS.

A Collection of the newest cotillions and country dances.
Worcester, 1800. [A piracy of Griffiths 1794,
reprinted from the *Sky Lark,* 1797, with its six additional dances; plus thirty dances from John Bur-
bank's *New Collection,* Brookfield, 1799.]
AAS, NYPL.

After 1800, the reprints and piracies cease, for
the dances popularized by Griffiths had merged
into the general tradition. So many of them are
scattered through *A Select Collection,* Otsego,
1808, that it would be more to the point for the
curious to list the ones left out than all those put
in. It is pleasant to report that Griffiths' own
invention, "Griffiths' Fancy," had a long run.

Unlike the American Revolution, the French
Revolution was cultural and affected all dancing
profoundly. The enormous hoops and headdresses
of the old regime were swept away in a fervor of
fashion, a reaffirmation of the human form, which
went as close as it decently could to the ideal of
Greek nudity. The result was the charming "chemise gown," a simple tube of muslin or other soft
material, cut low at the neck and girded high
beneath the bosom. A single garment underneath
was deemed quite enough, with a shawl for out-
of-doors. The girls swore they weren't cold,
although young Charlotte (in the old American

ballad) froze stiff in the sleigh on the way to a
ball. The men's nether garments were reduced to
skin-tights. Then, when the Reign of Terror ended
with the fall of Robespierre on July 27, 1794,
France was swept with a mania for balls, — the
dance of Life at the passing of the shadow of
imminent Death.

And how they could dance in their simplified
costumes! The music speeded up, leaving little
time for the more complicated elegances of
deportment. In the Christmas Eve dance at Brace-
bridge Hall, Irving described the discomfiture of
the old style when it met the new.

> Master Simon, who seemed to be a kind of connecting link
> between the old times and the new, and to be withal a little
> antiquated in the taste of his accomplishments, evidently
> piqued himself on his dancing, and was endeavoring to gain
> credit by the heel and toe, rigadoon, and other graces of the
> ancient school; but he had unluckily assorted himself with a
> litttle romping girl from boarding-school, who, by her wild
> vivacity, kept him continually on the stretch, and defeated all
> his sober attempts at elegance.

The craze spread instantly to America. Only
one dancebook had been published here before
1794; thirty that we know of appeared, mostly in
Puritan New England, before the end of the
century: at Northampton and Greenfield in 1794;
at Walpole, (N.H.) in 1795; at Philadelphia,
Hanover, Boston, and Baltimore in 1796; at Hartford, Baltimore, Rutland and Worcester in 1797;

at Philadelphia, Amherst, Brookfield, Norwich and Stonington-Port in 1798; at Philadelphia, Walpole (N.H.), New Haven, Hartford, Brookfield, Leominster, Newport, and Boston in 1799; at Worcester, New York, Harvard, and Philadelphia in 1800.[18] There may have been as many again, which were used to bits, then thrown away without leaving any traces for the bibliographer.

The French squares were increasing in popularity, in spite of the fact that they were both complicated and short. The first difficulty was got over by giving the dancers printed directions (as they did at Almack's);[19] and playing cards with these directions have been preserved. Fans on which the steps and music of the new dances were printed became fashionable in England in 1797. The second difficulty was not got over so easily. Why bother to learn something which was finished as soon as four couples had done their bit, while the simpler contras lasted until the twenty or so couples had danced? But after 1800, the dancing-masters worked out a sequence of "changes" — all hands round, balance partners, grand right and left, and so forth — which sequence the dancers memorized once and for all. Then these "changes" were danced as though

[18] See "American Dance Bibliography to 1820," *Proceedings of the American Antiquarian Society,* LIX, 217-20, Worcester, 1950.

[19] Pierce Egan, *Life in London,* London [1821], pp. 309-10.

they were the verses of a song, with the "figure" (or cotillion proper) taking the place of the chorus. Thus the cotillion was made to last about as long as the country-dance.

These changes appear first in *Mr. Francis's Ball Room Assistant*, Philadelphia, [1801]. "Saltator's" *Treatise on Dancing*, Boston, 1802, lists ten changes; *A Selection of Cotillons & Country Dances*, [Boston], 1800, lists only seven; but Willard Blanchard's *Collection of the most Celebrated Country Dances and Cotillions*, Windsor, 1809, lists fourteen.

The device was ingenious, but died out when calling was invented. The "changes" survive as the introductory part of almost every square-dance of today; but the word itself is now applied to the dance proper.

It was the War of 1812 which ensured the popularity and development of the square-dance in this country. The pro-English New Englanders kept on with the English contras, and indeed invented one of the best, "Hull's Victory," to celebrate the great victory of the "Constitution" over the "Guerriere" on August 19, 1812.[20] But

[20] Known tactfully in Canada as "The Halls of Victory," and as "Hell's Victory" in those parts of our West where our naval history means little. In the *Community Dance Manual,* II, 2, July, 1948, of the English Folk Dance and Song Society, "Hull's Victory" is first in a list of "Five English-American Dances," with the astounding and completely unsupported statement that "These dances are of British origin, carried to America." The other four

the rest of the nation refused to dance the English
dances, and would do nothing but the French
squares, as various English travellers noted with
contempt.

At this point, some smart American invented
"calling," which made it unnecessary to memorize
the dance beforehand. Like all great inventions,
it was simple: the fiddler or the leader of the
orchestra merely kept telling the dancers what to
do next. Nobody who knew the six or eight
fundamental calls could go very far wrong. The
fiddler thus ceased to be an accompanist: he
became the creator of the dance. He could vary
the figures at any moment, just to keep the dancers
on their toes; he could invent new dances; he could
even call at random anything that happened to pop
into his head. These "fancy-figures," when nobody
knew what was coming next, became popular as
the last dance in a "sett." The prompter could
and eventually did sing the calls, weaving rude
rhymes, and filling out the calls with comments on
the individuals present. Thus the ancient trio of
melody, verse, and dance was identified once more;
and the caller was the modern equivalent of the

are "Irish Trot, or Thady You Gander," "Portland Fancy,"
"Firemens Dance," and "Washington Quickstep." Since writing
this note, I have been told that "Hull's Victory" was an adapta-
tion of a Scottish dance. The Duchess of Gordon is said to have
introduced Scottish dances to English society about the turn of
the century.

antique *choragus*. But most important of all: he kept square-dancing alive, fluid, growing, at the very time it was becoming formalized in Europe.[21]

In France, the craze for new cotillions wore itself out, and the best five or six of them were organized into a suite called "the quadrilles." Lady Jersey introduced the suite at Almack's in 1815, where immediately it swept all the old cotillions into

---

[21] An American dancing - master evidently tried to introduce calling in London. Thomas Wilson, ballet master of the King's Theater, mentions him in *The Danciad,* London, 1824, p. 11, a satire against rival dancing-masters:

> With nasal twang, I heard this creature call
> The quadrille figures at his last grand ball.

The words which Wilson italicized indicate his victim's nationality.

The first reference to calling in this country, as far as we know, occurs in *Travels through North America, During the Years* 1825-1828 by Bernard, Duke of Saxe-Weimar-Eisenach, Philadelphia, 1828, I, 212; he attended a ball at Columbia, S. C., where the figures were called by a fiddler.

Mrs. Trollope (*Domestic Manners of the Americans,* London, 1832, I, 214) remarked that calling "has a very ludicrous effect on European ears."

Fanny Kemble (*Journal,* Philadelphia, 1835, I, 243) described with lively disgust the "fancy figures" improvized at the close of almost every quadrille.

Dickens actually records the calls for a quadrille in a London underworld dance-hall run by and for negroes (obviously American ones) in "Poor Mercantile Jack" (*All the Year Round, II,* 464, March 10, 1860; collected in the *Uncommercial Traveller*). Dark Jack's calling is filled with lively interjections and exhortations and even shouts; and the blacks dance with a vigorous style unknown to the London parlor: "They toed and heeled, shuffled, double-shuffled, double-double-shuffled, covered the buckle, and beat the time out rarely."

Douglas and Helen Kennedy, in *Square Dances of America,* Wessex Press, England [1931?], p. 4, state: "One characteristic feature that America has added to these old dance forms lies in the "calling."

"Call" in this sense, does not appear in Murray's *New English Dictionary.*

oblivion. Now one needed memorize only these
particular figures. In this country it was called the
"French Quadrille" or the "Plain Quadrille"; it is
still danced occasionally, though much changed
by time, and I think improved.

The French Quadrille was still rural in senti-
ment: the figures were named "Pantalon," "L'Été,"
"La Poule," "Pastourelle" (substituted for the earlier "Trénis) and "Finale."[22] The original music
was soon lost, as every composer of popular music
wrote new suites for the dance, each section being
labeled "Pantalon" and so on.

Quadrilles and cotillions are often confused.
The difference is that which lay between the
increasingly elegant city and the still roisterous
country-side. In the quadrilles, the sequence of
figures was fixed and therefore memorized. The
cotillions might be put together anyhow into a
"sett," as long as the last figure was a lively "jig"
or "breakdown"; they were not memorized but
called. Quadrille music was art-music (indeed,
the latest grand operas were regularly pillaged for
the melodies) while the cotillions clung to the

---

[22] The *Grande Encyclopedie*, XIII, 873, states that the first
figure was danced to a very old air, "Le pantalon de Toinon n'a
pas du fond"; "L'Ete" was a very complicated dance of 1800,
of which only the title was kept; "La Poule" was a contredanse
of Julien, 1802, the second part of the tune representing the cluck-
ing of a hen; the "Trenis" was invented by a celebrated dancer
and named for him; the "Pastourelle," which replaced it, was
based on village airs; and the "Finale," which was very fast,
came to be called the "galop."

traditional folk-tunes. The quadrilles aimed at
deportment, the cotillions at exercise. The quadrilles were therefore considered *haute école,* in
contrast to the elemetary cotillions.

Fanny Wright gives us a glimpse of affairs here
before the quadrille took over too completely.

> The fashions here are copied from the French . . . The
> dances too, (and these young women, as far as my judgment
> may go with you for anything, dance with as much lightness,
> grace, and gay-heartedness,) the dances are also French,
> chiefly quadrilles;[23] certainly prettier to look at than the
> interminable country-dance, whose appalling column seems to
> picture out some vague image of space and time which the
> imagination cannot see the end of . . . .

> [In winter] the light *sleighs,* peopled with the young and
> gay, bound along to the chime of bells, which the horses seem
> to hear well pleased. In country and city, this is the time
> of amusement; the young people will run twenty miles,
> through the biting air, to the house of a friend; where all in
> a moment is set astir; carpets up, music playing, and youths
> and maidens, laughing and mingling in the mazy dance, the
> happiest creatures beneath the moon.[24]

On lower social levels, "junkets" might be called
on the inspiration of the moment. Everything,
including the stove, was lugged out of the kitchen;
the fiddler was perched in the sink; and to the old
tunes the old contras and cotillions were per-

---

[23] Miss Wright, writing for the English, used "quadrilles"
where an American would have written "cotillions";   English
travellers were always complaining that the Americans misnamed
the quadrilles.

[24] [Frances Wright], *Views of Society and Manners in America
. . . during the years* 1818, 1819, *and* 1820, New York, 1821,
pp. 27, 331.

formed, with the old vigor. When new songs scored hits (particularly those of Stephen Foster), the better callers invented dances for them, which insensibly adapted themselves to the structure of the song: introduction, four stanzas, chorus, and sometimes a coda. (Thus the form of the modern square came into existence.) But in the city, things were different. There they glided through the latest quadrilles from abroad, with more and more elegance and languor. Thackeray found them "dreary as a funeral."[25] Dickens looked back to the fun that used to be when he described the quadrille at Signor Billsmethi's Dancing Academy: "None of your slipping and sliding about, but regular warm work, flying into corners, and diving among chairs, and shooting out the door, — something like dancing![26] When this old-time heartiness had subsided into mere deportment, the youngsters enthusiastically let off steam in the polka, which reached England in 1844 and was promptly banned (in vain) by Queen Victoria and by the Empress Eugénie.

For the introduction of the quadrille marked the return to the lilies and languors. The new decorum was soon reflected in the styles for women. About 1825, the chemise - gown went out of fashion.

[25] *Mrs. Perkins's Ball,* London, 1847.

[26] "The Dancing Academy," *Bell's Life in London,* II, 158-170, Oct. 11, 1835; collected in *Sketches by Boz.*

Waist and skirt became separate garments again, and petticoats returned and multiplied. Crinoline, an expensive material of horse-hair, was used to stiffen out the skirts. Carrying all this load, the ladies affected a "delicacy" which soon became real. Out of doors they heavily veiled their complexions against the dreaded rays of the sun; indoors, they wore gloves. Tuberculosis spread; they blamed it on the scanty garments of their girlhood.

But the tremendous drive into the West preserved the old-style dances in their original vigor. The emigrants took these dances with them; balls became the chief means of getting the scattered settlers together and preserving their sanity. These balls "could be a riotous revel that attracted people from many miles about and that lasted through the night if not through the entire week." [27] If there were no white women, squaws did very well. At Fort Union in September, 1857, the Swiss artist Rudolph Friederich Kurz watched the Indian women going through the cotillions (which were the favorite dance) "with much more grace and far more correctness than I would have expected."[28] The forty-niners in California did not even have squaws; nor did they need them, for these dances (be it repeated) were games, not

[27] Marshall B. Davidson, *Life in America,* Boston, 1951, II, 12.

[28] Rudolph Friederich Kurz, *Journal,* Washington, 1937, p. 125.

courtship. The men with conspicuous patches on their seats were automatically the ladies, a fact which accounts for the popular last call: "Promenade to the bar and treat your partners."[29] In such rowdy circumstances the western style of square-dancing originated.

Switching back from the Pacific to the Atlantic coast, we find the climax of Victorianism in the "Lancers," the most fashionable quadrille of the half century. It was popularized in 1856 by the Empress Eugénie, who in the same year reintroduced the hoop-skirt, to conceal her pregnancy.

The Lancers was the nineteenth-century equivalent of the minuet. It was all bows and courtesies, airs and graces, an elegant exhibition of deportment. There was nothing in it which could put the most delicate lady in the slightest glow. Originally it had been an English dance, which went unvalued until the French toned it down and polished it up.[30] It set a style; there were many

[29] *Harper's Weekly,* I, 634, Oct. 3, 1857, "Mining Life in California." The author does not name the dances but mentions the calls "Ladies' Chain" and "Set to your partners." Stewart Edward White, in *The Westerners,* 1901, Ch. 30, describes a ball at which only two girls are present; the last call is "All promenade to th' bar!" One recalls also the impromptu men's Virginia Reel in Owen Wister's *Virginian,* and the ball at which the hero changes all the sleeping children about.

[30] It was named for the lancers of the regiment at Fontainebleau, who thereafter were admitted to all the balls. The music came from England. The first number was by Paolo Diana Spagnoletti (1768-1834), conductor at the King's Theater for thirty years; the second came from the opera *Lodoiska* (1791) by

imitations, some of them quite successful; but the original Lancers outlived them all, except the 'Loomis Lancers," invented by the New Haven dancing-master, which is still done in Rhode Island and southern Massachusetts.

During the next generation there was a silent war between the dancing-masters determined to preserve and improve the French decorums and the youngsters determined to get exercise.

First of all, the teachers proclaimed that "doing one's steps" was now vulgar. One might walk or glide; that was all. No more in the "Pastourelle" of the French Quadrille was the "cavalier seul" to caper before his partner,[31] nor, in its expansion, the "Cauliflower Cotillion," could his partner respond. No more could that expert dancer Ichabod Crane clatter his loose frame about the room, to the delight of the darkies; nor might Mr. Fezziwig "cut" so deftly that he appeared to wink with his legs. Gone were the didoes that took both strength and skill: the ballotes, the pas de Basque, the vaults and pirouettes, entre-chats, rigadoons, pas de

Rudolph Kreutzer, to whom Beethoven dedicated a sonata; the third was an old folk-tune used in the *Beggar's Opera* (1728); the fourth has not been traced; the fifth was by Felix Janiewicz (1762-1848), a Polish violinist, and an original member of the London Philharmonic Society.

[31] Compare Jerry "sporting a toe" at Almack's in Pierce Egan's *Life in London* (1821), with the solemn Bob Hely, depicted by Thackeray in *Mrs. Perkins's Ball* (1847), who is performing the same figure without the steps.

bourrée, petits battements, and jetés,—all the "pas
this and pas that and pas t'other" which had
distressed Bob Acres a century before.[32]

[32] In 1802, "Saltator" said: "The quantity of steps used in
dancing is almost innumerable" (*Treatise on Dancing*, Boston
1802, p. 54). However, as dancing speeded up, the number dimi-
nished. The anonymous *Selection of Cotillons & Country-Dances*,
[Boston], 1808, tried to cut the number down to a fundamental
eight, but mentioned others which were variations. The tendency
continued through the first half-century, but was pronounced a
principle only in the second half.

Elias Howe (*Howe's Complete Ball-Room Hand-Book, Boston,*
1858, p. 4) wrote: "In dancing let your steps be few, but well and
easily performed . . . preferring to lead your partner gracefully
through the figure, than by exhibiting your agility by a vigorous
display of your muscles, in the performance of an entrechat or a
pigeon's wing, which may do very well for a hornpipe, but would
be quite out of place in a quadrille or cotillon."

Edward Ferrero (*The Art of Dancing*, New York, 1859, p. 121)
remarked that "the quadrille of former times was adopted as a
medium for the display of agility and the indulgence of violent
exercise," but now that the difficult steps had been abolished, anybody who knew the figures could do the dance.

Beadle's Dime Ball-Room Companion, New York, 1868, p.
16: "any attempt at 'doing your steps' [is] rigidly tabooed."

Wm. B. DeGarno (*The Dance of Society*, New York, 1875,
p. 13) opens his introduction by explaining that the steps of
stage-dancing are not now used in the ballroom.

C. H. Cleveland, Jr. (*Dancing at Home and Abroad*, Boston,
1878, pp. 34-5): "Never make 'clog-dance' or 'jig-' steps in a
parlor or ball-room. They may be very skilful and possibly (to
some) funny; but they are also rude and coarse. It has been
said "that a 'jig-tune' will bring out all the vulgarity at a ball."
[A jig-tune was the music for the last and quickest number in
a set].

How to Dance, New York, 1878, p. 10: "When passing through
a quadrille . . . avoid any display of agility or knowledge of steps."

However, prohibitions do not prohibit. Who could ever forget
Denman Thompson's terrific pigeon-wing in the Virginia Reel at
the end of the *Old Homestead?* Ira W. Ford (*Traditional Music
of America*, New York, 1940) translates "Balance all!" as "Execute
any few steps before swinging partners" (p. 198) and adds: "The
caller may shout 'Powder River!' at any time during the Grand
Right and Left. The dancers pause, cut the pigeon-wing, dance
a jig, or execute some special steps before swinging partners"

Next, the dictators of the dance decreed that country dances were no longer fashionable. This notion had started when the new skirts began to hang really heavy. At the Ladies' Seminary run by Mrs. Wackles (*Old Curiosity Shop*, 1840-41, ch. viii), "country-dances, being low, were utterly proscribed",[33] and in 1841 the *Ball Room Instructer* [sic] of New York announced that "quadrilles and cotillons have completely taken the place of all former dances which enlivened our ancestors." But not until the hoop-skirt had reached its full did the other dancing-masters chime in. Thomas Hillgrove remarked (*Complete Practical Guide*, New York, 1863, p. 230):

> Country dances have become nearly obsolete in fashionable assemblies, but are still in comparative favor at provincial balls and private parties. They belong to a ruder age than ours, and were relished by a merrier people than now move in the circles of fashion; they are characteristic of Merry England in the olden time — of the cheerful, gay, and lighthearted, but hold an inferior place in the programme of a modern assembly.

> (p. 199). A return to this tradition is to be found in the "Double Do-Si-Do," chosen as the "dance of the month" in the *New England Caller* (I, vii, 25) for February 1952: "At the call Hi-De-Ho, the dancers are encouraged to wriggle shake, strut a bit, do the Charleston, or anything else they want — or just shout Hide-ho along with the caller."

[33] "Doing one's steps" was still in style, however, for in the quadrille the slightly inebriated Dick Swiveller "performed such feats of agility and such spins and twirls" that Mrs. Wackles momentarily revised her disapproval of this "gay young man" and began to think that "to have such a dancer as that in the family would be a pride indeed."

He then gives directions for Money Musk, Chorus Jig, and College Hornpipe, but refuses to give more, "as they are no longer fashionable." Wm. B. DeGarno (*The Dance of Society*, New York, 1875, p. 50) is equally condescending. Under "Contra Dances" he describes the Spanish Dance and the Sicilian Circle (two progressive circles) and "Sir Roger de Coverly, known in America as the Virginia Reel"; he warns his reader, however, that "they are not considered fashionable, yet are more or less done all over the country." And thus, with the contras technically eliminated, the word "square-dances" began to be used.[34]

New England characteristically gave no ear at all to these snobbish fiats. Elias Howe's *Complete Ball-Room Hand-Book*, Boston, 1858, included 83 contras; his *American Dancing Master*, Boston, 1862, 110 contras; and his *Musician's Omnibus*, Boston 1864, 114. There were rival publications, which we need not list. To shift from New England, J. A. French's *Prompter's Handbook*, New York, c. 1893, describes thirty-six, explaining

[34] *Beadle's Dime Ball-Room Companion*, New York, c. 1868, uses "Square Dances" as a heading. E. B. Reilley, *The Amateur's Vade Mecum*, Philadelphia, 1870, p. 127, says: "Square Dances constitute now, as they ever have and probably ever will, the chief of social dances." Allen Dodsworth, *Dancing*, New York, 1885, p. 79, refers to the "so-called square dances." Playford, two centuries before, used the term "Square-Dance" (in which couples danced with their opposites) in contrast to "Round for 8" (in which one danced with one's corner).

that "only a few of the most popular contra dances will be given. A legion of old ones may be found in old violin books." Indeed, so often do the novels about old-time New England mention contras as to give the impression that the Yankees never danced anything else.

Meanwhile the city youngsters were protesting against the dullness of the quadrilles The formula (the head couples did a figure, which was repeated by the side couples, the whole then being done all over again) could be cut in half by forming squares of two couples only, or by straightening out the square into two lines of four each. Often two or three of the five figures were omitted. But better yet: waltzes or polkas were woven in at the end of each figure, a practice so popular that the Congress of the Episcopal Church in America debated in 1877 whether or not to ban all square-dancing (hitherto the bulwark against the wicked round dances) because they now had "a resistless tendency to round off into the waltz."[35] The Episcopalians decided, however, that it was a matter of taste and not of morals, so the ban was not passed.

The "lascivious" waltz had long been looked at askance. Actually to clasp a girl close in your arms and then revolve dizzyingly seemed to many

[35] *Harper's Magazine,* LIX, 302-3, Jan. 1878. The matter, it seems, had also been brought up in the Congress at Washington.

people the depth of wickedness. There were such
possibilities of contact! Club-foot Byron's vulgar
satire is known to scholars, but the same thing is
said more neatly in the following poem from a
Vermont songster of 1815:

What! the Girl I adore, by another embraced?
What! the balm of her lip shall another Man taste?
What! touch'd in the twirl, by another Man's knee?
What! panting recline, on another than me?
—Sir, she's yours—from the Grape you have press'd the
   soft blue.
From the Rose, you have shaken the tremulous dew.
What you've *touch'd* you may *take!* — Pretty Waltzer
   —Adieu.[36]

The next year, 1816, the popular Emperor
Alexander of Russia made the waltz socially
acceptable by dancing it publicly in Paris and
London; but even his imperial prestige could not
quell the qualms of those who had never waltzed;
and to this day, waltzing is banned by certain
sects. The youngsters, of course, adored it the
more.

By the 1870's, the nadir of "delicacy" was
passed. Hoops shrank to bustles; croquet, followed
by lawn tennis, gave the girls something like out-
of-door exercise. But their chief exercise still took
place on the dance-floor. It was in this situation
that some Yankee invented "swinging," which
revolutionized square-dancing in the north-east.

[36] *Songster's Companion,* Brattleborough, 1815, p. 213.

"Swinging," in the old dance-books, meant simply joining hands with one's partner, and revolving once around. In the parlor "carpet quadrilles," nothing could be more decorous; but in the kitchen junket or barn dance, one went around twice, in a brief burst of speed that momentarily caught something like the whirl of the waltz.

And now the anonymous Yankee invented a new grip, which made the dangerous contacts of the waltz impossible, also a new position of the feet.[37] The result was the "buzz step." Never before had dancers twirled so rapidly. It was bacchanalian, a terpsichorean cocktail. It was such fun, one did it, not once or twice, but as long as the music allowed. It invaded all squares (except the formal quadrilles) and some contras. Dances like the "Spanish Cavalier" (the music is dated 1878) consisted of little else, being devised to make the girls dizzy. I may add, they like it.

[37] Left hands were joined (thus keeping a fist between the couple) ; right hands were placed on opposite right shoulders (thus strong-arming the partner away) ; and the two leaned away from each other, to get the full advantage of centrifugal force. (Later, in many places, the waltz position was used.) Meanwhile the right feet were placed outside each other, the little toes almost touching; then one revolved on the right foot, using the left to propel one, much like a kid on a scooter.

The earliest reference which I have found to this modern step occurs in a song, "Dancing in the Barn," by Turner, Orrin, and McKee, New York, c. 1878:

> Den swing your partners all together,
> Kase now's the time for you to learn.

Modern swinging, be it noted, is the only square-dance step which requires practice.

Swinging to the buzz step is still unknown in parts of the south and the west, though in a few years it should be universal.

It also seems to be about the 1870's that singing calls began to be common. Even before calling came in, the fiddler at an informal dance could do something towards directing it. The colored musician at the quilting frolic in Irving's "Legend of Sleepy Hollow" is described as "bowing almost to the ground and stamping with his foot whenever a new couple was to start." At the Dingley Dell ball, which Mr. Pickwick opened with Mrs. Wardle, the first fiddler also stamped to indicate when a new couple became active. After calling was invented, the ordinary leader was content to "prompt" the dancers by naming the next step. When the prompter began to improvise patter is not known, but it must have been long before a patter-call actually found its way into *Howe's Complete Ball-Room Hand Book* (1858), where it may be found in the "Punch and Judy Set" (pp. 52-3). I quote from the second number.

First lady balance to right hand gentleman, swing the gentleman with big feet — pass on and balance to the next gentleman, swing the gentleman with the long nose — pass on and balance to the next gentleman, swing the gentleman with the red hair—balance to partners, swing the best looking gentleman in the set . . .

After this, the time was bound to come when the caller actually sang to the music, filling out with

extra words or nonsense syllables. The earliest
reference I have found to this practice occurs in
Hamlin Garland's recollections of his boyhood —
about 1870 — in *A Son of the Middle Border*
(New York, 1917, p. 94):

> At this dance I heard, for the first time, the local profes-
> sional fiddler, old Daddy Fairbanks . . . His queer "Calls"
> and his "York State" accent filled us all with delight. *"Ally*
> man left," "Chassay *by* your pardners," "Dozy-*do*" were some
> of the phrases he used as he played *Honest John* and *Haste
> to the Wedding.* At times he sang his calls in high nasal
> chant, *"First* lady lead to the *right,* deedle, deedle dum-dum
> —*gent* foller after after—dally-deedle-do-do—*three* hands
> round"—and everybody laughed with frank enjoyment of his
> words and action.

It is impossible to guess how long this practice had
been going on without being mentioned in print.[38]
The dancing-masters, of course, sternly ignored

[38] In Mary Wilkins Freeman's *Madelon* (New York, 1896,) a
novel about a New England town in the early nineteenth century,
the heroine, in the absence of the usual fiddler, is persuaded to
"lilt" the tunes, which she does "in a curious disyllabic fashion."
This would seem to be the Irish lilting of tunes on meaningless
syllables, without using the calls. If so, this is the first instance
of an Irish influence on American dancing, — a rare event, as
the Irish usually excluded all others from their dances, and thus
neither influenced nor were influenced.
   At any rate, Madelon's lilting was different from the practice
of simply getting the girls to sing in such an emergency (Ann S.
Stephens, *Old Homestead,* Philadelphia, 1885, p. 366). The sects
which prohibited all instrumental music considered a dance not a
sinful dance but an innocent game when the spectators sang and
clapped. Hamlin Garland (*A Son of the Middle Border,* p. 184)
describes such an occasion, when "Weevily Wheat" was performed. But the words he records do not include the calls.
   In Act III of Belasco's *May Blossom,* (c. 1883) the dancers
themselves break out into singing the calls, but this probably was
only a dramatic effect.

these unseemly gyrations and vocalizings amongst
the lower-class indelicates, and continued to look
to Paris for the latest quadrilles. But now Paris
began to look at America. As early as 1857, the
famous Cellarius, with the aid of one J. Martin,
had contrived a lively "quadrille gallope" called
"L'Américain," in which the couples were renum-
bered counter-clockwise (American style?) instead of by opposites. But not until 1880 (or
perhaps a year or so earlier) did Monsieur Fr. Paul
create "Polo, le quadrille américaine," the third
great quadrille, based on American figures. It was
a sensation. French-poodled though it was, the
inherent vigor of the dances could not be repressed.
At private parties, the music was played faster
than indicated, and the squares whirled until the
ladies' coiffures came to pieces. Consequently it
could not be performed at the grand balls, and it
did its bit in confirming the European belief that
the Americans were a wild bunch. Today it seems
tame enough. Its ingredients were rudiments of
our "Back to Back," "Forward Up Six," "Grande
Allemande," the old "Basket Cotillion," and what
we now call the "Texas Star."[39]

[39] French dance-books have not been generally available to
me, but I can call attention to J. Lagus's *Nouveau Guide des
Danses Francaises* & *Americaines* (Paris, ca. 1888?) which in-
cludes a "schottische americain," "La The York" (which American
amateurs had popularized), "Polo," and a "noveau quadrille americain."

By the 1890's, square-dancing was rapidly ebb-
ing from the sight of city society. The sad story of
its decline may be traced in the *Galop* (1884-97),
the first American magazine devoted to the dance.
As the organ of the American National Associa-
tion of Masters of Dancing (organized 1883), it
was naturally conservative, and indeed could
scarcely have worked harder to destroy the very
thing it was trying to further. It attacked swinging, of course. It also attacked calling, because
ladies and gentlemen should know the standard
dances by heart. It could get positively libellous
against the uncouth non-members of the associa-
tion. An article, "Prompters," in the number for
October 1893, attacks these independents bitterly.
The prompter, "or as styled in some places a figure
caller or caller-off" is generally "a very poor
musician, with a 'big voice,' who has got all his
knowledge from cheap handbooks.

Many of these "figure callers" after a time compose new
and original figures to suit their own peculiar views. It is
little wonder that quadrilles have been driven out of society,
when they had to be performed under the tutelage of these
worthies, for when the mixing-up process is applied in full
force of the prompter, the ablest mind-reader on earth
would be thrown into utter despair while endeavoring to
conjecture what might follow in the line of figures, in any
number of a quadrille, as the most outlandish and seemingly
inconceivable movements are frequently demanded, while
even the standard figures are not infrequently despoiled.

It has been a governing rule in dancing from time immem-
orial, that a turn should be made as a finishing part of a

balance . . . while, of course, the turn should be made with
the person to whom the balance has been made . . . For
some unaccountable reason, the prompters have made a sad
change in this, as invariably the order goes; balance corners—
swing partners—thus perpetrating a gross breach of etiquette;
almost as direct a cut at it would be to extend the hand to
a person to shake hands (as a token of welcome), then
to immediately turn away and shake the hand of another
person . . .

. . . Ask them why they use the term *swing* instead of *turn*
and they generally answer with a very intelligent *grin*. In
fact, that is the only form of reply they can make, for they
cannot answer otherwise intelligently . . .

In what seems to have been the last number of
the *Galop* (1897, vol. xiv, no. 1 — no month
given) is a dismal editorial "Whither Are We
Going?" In the 50's, 60's and 70's, society danced
"Quadrille, Lanciers, Portland Fancy, Money
Musk, Chorus Jig, The Merry Dance, Waltz,
Schottische, Polka, Galop, Varsouvienne, Mazurka,
Redowa Polka, Danish Dance, Petronella, Spanish
Dance, etc., etc., etc." But now little is done but
the round dances, and these have dwindled to the
Waltz and Galopade, "or, as more familiarly
known the 'Two Step.' When this movement was
revived a few years ago on the Bowery, to six-
eight time, a complete revolution in the dancing
world was inaugurated." Another gloomy item
lists the dancing-masters who have returned to
their former callings — barber, printer, waiter,
farmer—and concludes: "Stick to the '*lone waltz*'

if you will, dear boys, but it means — 'Over the hill to the poorhouse'."

The dancing-schools, then, were the last stronghold of square-dancing in the cities. When I was a boy in the 1890's, I learned the "Lancers" and a couple of other quadrilles, the "Portland Fancy," the "Paul Jones," and the imperishable "Virginia Reel," besides the waltz, the "barn dance" (Military Schottische), and the two-step. (The two-step was an American dance, invented to go with the Sousa marches; it was characterized by a little spring on the offbeat before the first slide — a lightness which differentiated it from the dragging polka step.) But when I graduated from dancing-school to regular balls, nothing was danced but waltzes and two-steps.

In fact, all over Europe as well, the ancient folk-dances were dying out. The peasants now preferred modern dress and waltzes to their traditional costumes and dances. In various countries, societies were formed to record and encourage their treasures of national culture. Cecil J. Sharp in 1905, found a couple of old men who still remembered the Morris Dance; he brought them to London, where they taught it to a girls' club, whose exhibition the following year started a revival which is still continuing. Mr. Sharp also recovered and interpreted Playford's old book in its various editions, thus adding to the repertory of old English dances.

Three years before the Morris was exhibited in London, a parallel movement was started in America, but with this great difference (incredible in any other country!) that it imported foreign folk-dances instead of seeking out the native. In 1903, Dr. Luther H. Gulick, the newly appointed athletic director of the schools in greater New York, decided that dancing was more fun than dumb-bells, and set a hundred thousand boys to learning European folk-dances. In a very few years, they were in the curriculum for girls as well as boys. Thanks to American enthusiasm and efficiency, the movement spread rapidly through the schools and colleges of many big cities. The English dances arrived in 1911. Soon May festivals and other celebrations attracted huge crowds to the playgrounds and parks, where the children and a few older groups put on their show. It was prophesied confidently that within a generation these foreign dances would become a permanent part of our melting-pot culture.

Of course, nothing of the sort happened. The movement did introduce some excellent singing games into the kindergartens and lowest grades. But the high hopes of the movement were never fulfilled; and with the advantage of hindsight, we can now see why.

In the first place, the movement was aimed primarily at children; consequently most grown persons could not be persuaded to "do kid stuff." Secondly, the peasant dances pleaded for peasant costumes, particularly in the public exhibitions; and as the little boys wouldn't dress up, the bigger girls had to take their places. Thirdly, the teachers turned these games into drills. It was down in the book how it had to be done. But worst of all, the native American dances, which should have been the foundation of the whole thing, were ruled out with tacit unanimity. Even the Virginia Reel was excluded. I suppose they were not considered "educational"; or, being our own, were aesthetically inferior. Yet almost in the backyards of the cities were the contras and squares which had died out in Europe, not to mention a big repertoire of original ones.

As the movement faded away, it was replaced for a time by Isadora Duncan's bare-foot dancing. This permitted spontaneity and creativeness; but it was "aesthetic," and again the lads held aloof.[40]

40 Miss Duncan's dances, based on Greek sculpture, were world-wide in influence. In Russia, her spontaneity released the Russian ballet from the bonds of French convention, and started it on its dazzling career. Other American dancers were Loie Fuller, whose enormous swirling draperies were illuminatetd by electric lights

Presently a new spate of fancy dances drove out the stock waltzes and two-steps from the ballrooms. The "Turkey Trot" of 1912 was fun and easy; it was followed by the "Bunny Hug," the "Castle Walk," the Grapevine," the "Lame Duck," and many others. The only two which survive are the "Fox Trot" (named for Harry Fox) and the "Lindy Hop" (now called "jitter-bugging"). Square-dancing had apparently gone forever; actually, it was still going on, just out of sight of the summer boarders and across the continent.[41]

Because this activity went almost unrecorded, we should salvage the following poem from the *Two Step* (V, 99), March 1898:

AN IDAHO BALL

Git yo' little sage hens ready,
Trot 'em out upon the floor—
Line up there, you cusses! Steady!

from below; Ruth St. Denis, re-creator of oriental dances; Ted Shawn, restorer of virility to the dance; Maude Allen, one of the earliest Salomes; and Martha Graham.

[41] A few glimpses are enough to prove its continuity.
H. C. Verner's song "Matilda," Chicago, 1896, starts:
"I met Matilda first one night when at a village dance,
Where all the boys for miles around stood waiting for a chance.
They started in with Money Musk, they danced with toe and heel,
And then I asked Matilda for the old Virginia Reel."
C. E. Ward's "Cowboy Songs and Dances" (*Pearson's Magazine*, Jan. 1903) is valuable for containing accurate transcriptions of the calls for "Split the Ring," "Birdie in a Cage," and others.
Ralph D. Paine's "An Old-Fashioned Country Dance" (*Outing* Magazine, Dec. 1905) describes an annual June junket somewhere in New York state, which began in mid-afternoon and continued fourteen hours till dawn. The old-time vigor was unabated: couples occasionally crashed into the orchestra.

Lively now!   One couple more.
Shorty! shed that old sombrero,
   Bronco, douse that cigarette.
Stop that cussin,' Casimero,
   'Fore the ladies!   Now, all set!
S'lute your ladies, all together!
   Ladies opposite the same—
Hit the lumber with your leathers!
   Balance all, an' swing your dame!
Bunch the heifers in the middle;
   Circle stags and do-se-do!
Pay attention to the fiddle!
   Swing her round and off you go!
First four forward!   Back to places!
   Second fellow shuffle back!
Now you've got it down to cases—
   Swing 'em till their trotters crack!
Gents all right a-heel and toeing!
   Swing 'em, kiss 'em if you kin—
On to next and keep a-goin'
   Till you hit yer pards ag'in!
Gents to center; ladies round 'em,
   Form a basket; balance all!
Whirl yer gals to where you found 'em!
   Promenade around the hall!
Balance to your pards and trot 'em
   'Round the circle, double quick!
Grab an' kiss 'em while you've got 'em—
   Hold 'em to [you] if they kick!
Ladies left hand to your sonnies!
   Alaman! Grand right and left!
Balance all, an' swing yer honeys—
   Pick 'em up and feel their heft!
Promenade like skeery cattle—
   Balance all and swing yer sweets!
Shake yer spurs an' make 'em rattle!
   Keno! Promenade to seats.
This is solid truth — I have attended many a party in the
Cedar Brakes in Texas, where they called even worse than
this.
                                            R. L. R.

The fad of community pageants, which started before the first World War, made many youngsters aware for the first time that square-dancing existed. Those communities which used their own history for their pageants naturally included the dances, as pageants demand dancing, and they still had their callers and repertoires. The war itself began to persuade some cultured Americans that their country was not so bad after all. An "American Folk Dance Society" was formed in February, 1916. Two years later appeared Elizabeth Burchenal's *Twenty - Eight Contra - Dances, Largely from the New England States.* Apparently this was the first American book of the sort, which sought out the past, not in the interest of scholarly preservation, or with the purpose of improving the school curriculum, but with the simple intent of getting grown people to do the dances. Old fiddle-books, to be sure, were still in print; but they were a survival, not a revival.

In 1925, a photograph of Henry Ford cutting a caper made the front pages from coast to coast.[42] The man who had done more to change the face of America than any other living man also wanted to preserve its past; and in square-dancing he hoped to find something to counteract what he considered the evils of jazz.

[42] *Literary Digest,* LXXXVI, 38-40, August 15, 1925.

The publicity he furnished gave a great spurt to the revival. More societies were formed; more books and pamphlets of squares collected in this or that state were published. It was not until the 30's, however, that Lloyd Shaw, who had been teaching the foreign folk-dances to a group of young people in a Colorado high-school, started collecting the old cowboy dances. In order to avoid the monotony of the same figure being repeated four times, he invented the "Exhibition Square," in which each couple does a different dance, the unity of effect being preserved by keeping the same chorus. When his pupils first appeared in public in 1938, they were so successful that the enthusiastic audiences wanted to join in; and the next year his important first book appeared.

Then the second World War swept away our last romantic notions that Europeans were better than Americans; the nation worked together as never before; and again, as in 1651, the spirit of democracy rose from the folk into the ballrooms. Countryside and city were one again.

At the New York World Fair in 1940, Ed Durlacher directed the square-dancing. The big recording companies began publishing albums of square-dances, to meet the new demand. In the old days, local callers used sometimes to foregather for competitions; now the competition was nation-wide, through these same albums, because whoever recorded the best dances got the biggest royalties. As for the public, one did not have to hire a caller and a band and a hall any more: one needed only ten feet square of floor-space, a phonograph, and four willing couples.

It was also during this decade that a number of "little magazines" devoted to square-dancing began to appear.

When America became nationally conscious of its folk-dancing, it discovered that each little community had its own way of doing the traditional dances, just as each fiddler had his own way of playing the tunes. There was no standard, no book which stated what was correct; there was no right or wrong — there was only better or worse. In short, the tradition was living, and therefore could keep on growing.

In the over-all survey, three different styles emerged: the southern, the north-eastern, and the western.

The South concentrates on the circle-dances, the "running sets" as they call them. (In the north, they are called the "Soldier's Joy," and are used as mixers.) In 1916, Cecil J. Sharp discovered these circle-dances in Kentucky; in spite of French calls and Irish tunes, he supposed them to be very, very early English, apparently on the grounds that nothing like them had survived in England. Of course, they could not have existed before the invention of calling. The running set has no fixed pattern; all depends on what the caller thinks of next.

In the North-East, the squares are based on swinging, and include the noisy kick-balance. The contras also have been preserved; there are still communities which dance little else. Ralph Page, the expert caller, has done much to spread them; it is said that they are beginning to be found outside New England again.

In the West, the squares are faster than in the East, and are more complicated. Where the easterners would swing, the westerner is content with a do-pa-so.[43]. A number of other new figures would seem to have originated here.

But wherever it is found, the American square dance has grown from its historical roots into something like nothing to be found elsewhere in the world. It has the advantages of being both a survival (in the country) and a revival (in the city) — the living, free tradition of the one combined with the enthusiasm of the other. It is

---

[43] Originally miscalled a "do-si-do," it has acquired a variety of different names in the past few years. The step consists of a left-hand round your partner, right-hand round your corner, and repeat as long as the caller calls it.

living, in the sense that it is growing, developing. The variety of patterns is already extraordinary. Yet they all follow more or less the pattern of popular song; introduction, four stanzas, chorus, and an occasional coda. Where the old squares would combine a couple of motifs and call it a number, the modern square uses a single motif and develops it. The result is an artistic unity that did not exist before. And as the modern generation is frankly athletic, the dances are quite vigorous.

The modern set consists of only three of these vigorous dances: first, what might be called the breather; then the brisk; and finally the rowdy. This last dance used to be called the "jig" or the "break-down."

Because the sets themselves are so lively, the interpolated couple-dances are milder. The polka returned, but a gentle form has prevailed. The schottische came and went. Attempts to introduce foreign folk-dances have mostly failed, because never was there a generation less romantic, less desirous of being European; yet a few of these dances, like the "Gay Gordons," succeeded on their own merits. Meanwhile, a lot of new fancy-dances are being invented, which succeed or fail on their own merits. It the east, they make a faint pretense of being imported; in other parts they are brazenly American.

New square-dances appear constantly. It seems that as long as there are new song-hits, there will be new dances, for the patterns evolved from the six or eight fundamental calls seem inexhaustible.

Finally, square-dancing is spreading beyond our borders. One hears of it in London, Japan, Canada, the Bermudas, Paris. For square-dancing is greater than any one nation: it is democracy itself, in dance form. Can anybody think of a better way to spread the spirit of democracy in a world that needs it so badly?